Intangible Bonds

Aarun Tripathi

BookLeaf Publishing

Presentation by *BookLeaf Publishing*

Web: www.bookleafpub.com

E-mail: info@bookleafpub.com

ISBN: 9789357697019

First edition 2023

DEDICATION

To my family who I adore unconditionally.

You know who you are.

ACKNOWLEDGEMENT

I would like to acknowledge the extraordinary debt to my family; not the one where we're tied by blood relations, but the one who stumbled upon my path one-by-one. Without their unconditional support, I wouldn't develop the courage to be tolerant, to be bold, and to harbour the unwavering hope that I will lead a life that I can be proud of. As for the book cover, the indisputable credit goes to one of my dearest friends Frida Kaeubler-DeLong. Lastly, I would like to extend my sincerest thanks to all of my new friends that I've made in university and for their tremendous support.

PREFACE

"Migrating to Canada has given me a second chance to re-create myself; start thinking about what I want and how do I wish to lead my life rather than on what was considered ideal by others. Today I stand, on my own two feet, screaming that I am proud of the way I fought."

Why did we ever meet?

The spherical world moves so fast;
After years of seeking you stand before me at last;
The feeling was a lot more than I asked;
You'll always be in the present, never the past. Why
did we ever meet?
What did I do to deserve you?
Why, do you smile at me?
What did I do to earn it?
The way you walk is so light;
It's almost you were about to leap into a flight.
A spirit as free as a kite;
You won't even set down in the night.
So tiny, so small, so innocent;
Purity bursts from within you.
How can I ever be near you without tainting it? What
can I say, it is indeed true.

An alluring flower that should bloom;
All this is what I've seen it assumed;
I feel like I've set you to doom;
As all I have done is gloom.
I'll move the clouds and let you shine through. Don't
worry, there's no price to pay.
There's nothing I would refuse for you.
That's a promise that will glow by the day.
All I want now is to stand strong;
So that no one could do you any wrong.
That desire has nurtured all along.

In my heart is where it should belong.
Why did we ever meet?
What did I do to deserve you?
Why do you smile at me?
What did I do to earn it?
Stay the way you are... My little ray of sunshine...

My Unwavering Companion

I am as strong as sturdy as you need me to be;
You study on me, sit on me, lay down on me,
Unlike a therapist, I don't take a fee.
The sharp wooden corners at my ends guarantee,
That I will hurt the haters of thee.
Sure, some people may not see,
That you are like a turbulent but warm sea.

Trust me, you are not a burden.

When your tears touch my surface,
That is when I serve my purpose.
I calm you down when you're nervous,
I try to find peace in your life's circus,
To which the tickets are unavailable to purchase.
I may not provide you with the warmth of a furnace,
Day or night, I will always be in your service.

Trust me, you are not weak.

I come in all styles and shades, companies and colors,
But I don't come with any ulterior covers.
I am my stoic and solid self even around suckers;
You own up to yourself even around others.
People will accept you even if you're not full of
summers.
Even if the world throws you vicious vultures,

I believe you are not the type who shudders.

Trust me, you are invincible.

Sincerely,
Your reason behind your strength,
Your study desk

A Battle For The Centuries

We don't get to choose our parents,
Nor do we get to choose our gender,
At least, that's what I believed for all these years.
No one taught me how to be myself.
Instead, I was taught how to please others.
I was taught what to like;
I was taught what to do when I am happy;
Flash that beautiful smile.
I was taught what to do when I am sad;
Stop crying, you're braver than that.
I was taught to meet expectations.
Be a doctor, my biological family says.
I take a step forward each day, and realize,
How far I am from what I was taught.
I was taught to smile when I'm happy, but I cry.
To stop crying when I am sad, I get infuriated.
Asking for help will make me weak, I am not.
I was taught what it means to be straight, I am not.
How to be a girl, I am a man.
Society will find different ways to trample me.
Rising above the norm is considered being rebellious.
That's what the teenage phase is perceived to be.
What I believe for the teenage phase to be, is to fight
with zest.
Let blood splatter all over you,
Let the blame and accusations crush you,
Until your eyes open to have a good look at yourself
in the mirror,

To unleash the hidden strength in you; the instinct of
survival.
Plenty of people have been been raped,
More have been killed.
All because they could fight for the people of their
future;
To protect the aspiring leaders who see the world,
For what it's truly intended to be; free.
Now it's time for us to fight for our future leaders.

The only rule to follow as we embark on a battle for
the centuries is,
Be free, just like this condensed narrative.

Light Of The Night

With the emerging light of the night,
Adjacent to the dusk on the show;
Sometimes an arch of gleaming patches of white;
More in doubt, less we know;
Sometimes a shimmering hemisphere alongside murk;
Half cynical, half sentimentals;
Sometimes a sparkling out curve conquering the dark work;
Standing out stronger than all metals;
And sometimes a spherical speck with scanted smears,
Completed us and hovering our fears.

Please Wake Up

Every single piece of pure Mother Nature,
Flowing in through your quivering nostrils,
Is what makes you my saviour.
The inability to inhale, drives my spine with chills.
Your beaming smile;
Rising out of your trapped core hostile,
Gives birth to the person I am today.
Brother... please wake up... there is still so much I
wish to convey.

Firecrackers or Handcuffs?

A pair of bursting firecrackers changed my life,
A pair of handcuffs that caused a strife;
Rising differences between the two.
One sets you free into the peaceful sky navy blue;
One chains you into rigidity which unmasks the bitter true.
Whether you get them or not,
Is not worth a second thought.
You need to value what you have got.

That alone can keep you away from an iron rot.

A locker and A staircase from middle school

Separated by the gleaming blue oceans,
Events arising with their own notions,
Both caused a dramatic commotion.
When the clock ticked, a resulted explosion.
The reason was wavering devotion;
The lack of form in emotion.
Time passed and those events remained unspoken.

Somewhere deep down,
That feeling was vigorously swirling around.
Life was at its invisible countdown;
A few words between new friends caused a frown,
As it got deeper, slowly there was a growing breakdown.

A transpiring event at a staircase,
A transpiring event at a locker,
The two might not be at the same place,
But the fact remains that our hearts were in a race.
A fear that we both had to conquer,
But we chose our feelings to be slaughtered.
Skipping to the end is instinctual;
To protect ourselves from pain is habitual;
For the strength, we need to move ahead, it's crucial.
But all we are doing, is dragging on the continual.
Life is indeed cruel, but undeniably punctual.

When fate unfolded to bring us to the same space,
Our words unconsciously went to trace.
The memories that we eagerly tried to erase,
I went through hell to emerge with grace,
You remained in a desolate place.
You preferred for your feelings to not showcase,
You tried to maintain a straight face.
But in the end, your feelings chose you to embrace.

Astrology constricts us

A science that is neglected by the world,
A truth that would cause a swirl.
Which will remain hidden
As we are forbidden.
The Gods and planets that rule us,
Bury our emerging guts.
The humans that we are,
That fact is marked as a scar.
Seemingly powerful but trapped in a cell.
Nothing will change the inevitable: we will rebel.

Internal Resistance

Like all the elements that are in existence,
Mother Nature also gives birth to the vine fruits.
With quality refinement, they annihilate internal resistance.
They are deeply anchored by their roots,
Which explains their unwavering persistence.
As they take away our prudence in a series of timed loots,
Bombarding us with an irresistible urge to erase our distance,
We both become a part of an agonizing pursuit.

A gentle breeze

There was once a time when I wished to menace it;
To visualize my agony splattering all over the marble floor.
In a state of betrayal and despair, I was about to submit.
But instead began an unknown, an unspoken, an
irreversible war.
Mother Nature watched me, like she always did.
She sent me a gentle breeze to flush my misery and
tenderly forbid.
A set of footsteps conducted a sprinted prance,
And instilled her brightness before I had the chance.

A Moment Of Pride

Mom, what does it mean to love someone?
You ask as your eyes dangle on a thin thread.
I was sure this day would arrive, my son.
Come, sit down, and listen to the journey I've led.

A picture is worth a thousand words,
As the father of realism once coined.
Capturing my beloved's former essence on a canvas,
And displaying it for enthralled eyes to dwell,
Is the first of the several steps of atonement
A flock of released rustic dove birds,
Flew where the roaring red and the tender teal joined.
His powerful prose colored me anxious,
But his vivid views liberated me as well.
My memory thrives in every stolen moment.

He said I deserved more than everything.

He shone in the darkness with his zest.
A rooted gremlin tragically tore him from within,
With everything snatched, he wasn't blessed.
But the sultry and solace of the sun resided in his skin;
And the fire in him glowed and he emerged victorious.
While I flashed one face, like the Earth sees of the moon.
An indestructible smile that I believed no one could break,
Scared, that my hollow holes would be visible too soon,
My smile was my soldier, my shield, but also fake.
I am destined to live in murk, I remain inglorious.

He said I was the reason he was brave.

He wasn't always a man like your father,
He made a choice for himself, to be one.
He wasn't one, but today he is.

The strive it takes to be free and not be afraid,
Is a quality that he possessed.
He mustered up the courage to confess;
His feelings about me and his new identity.
My shield was shattered and wrecked,
I walked away from the girl I loved, leaving her behind,
And I rejected the man I saw that day.

But then he said, I deserve to remain in agony.

Opposites attract as everyone loves to harp,
But often forget that both need strength;
To love, to forgive, to unconditionally accept;
Not just the imperfections, but for who they are;
When you embrace someone, you embrace their choices.
I was trapped in the norms of the world,
Thinking that everything has to be perfect,
Believing that everything needs to have structure;
And one can only work with what they have,
And not aspire for something that isn't theirs.

But today, he says, you worked hard to be here.

Your eyes widen as you begin to process my story.
Let it sink in, let it evoke an emotion in heart.
Let it free, let it swirl around in all parts of you.
Do you still love her? Or do you love him? You ask.
I respond, I love him, even if I know I can't be with him.
That, my son, is my penance for my decision to walk away.
A decision I do not want you to make;
A decision that my parents also contributed to;
It was not a decision, I know that.
I cannot call it a mistake; it led me to you.

Mom, can I make a confession?
You ask as your eyes snap from the dangling thread.
I am – not walking away from the man I love, you don't question.
As a mother, I felt an inexplicable sense of pride,
As your courage to admit it, stemmed from my story of regret.

Bloom Of A Jonquil

Winter evokes the sense of ice cold columns;
Springtime kindles the rosy cherry blossoms;
Amidst these seasons a jonquil blooms in the rise.
Seasons change as this flower skies.
The drive to chase after the unthinkable,
Was indeed a surprise to my eyes.
The words on the page that flew to be visual;
Encircled around me and were no longer mythical.
Bringing them to life was the hope you shone upon me.
We will see, if you agree.

Power I Behold

Tremendous powers parents have piled;
Shattering the dreams of a child;
That tiny life that once smiled,
All feelings arose to be exiled.

Expression of my knitted ambition,
Paving future's path in my own direction,
Resulted in an immoral ignition,
Of your honorable position.

Tears dripped off my face;
Uncontrollable of its course,
Due to my failed chase,
Where I couldn't move past your force.

Not once did you embrace;
Not once did you show remorse,
When you stormed off the place,
Leaving me as a forsaken weak force.

The kitchen rested in front of my eyes,
The knife was right there, within my sight.
I wished to indefinitely put an end to my cries,
As the bright light seemed so bright.

On the knife my fingers came to a rest,
A tightening sensation was felt across my chest;
No one could have guessed,
That my existence depended on this one test.
This is the essence of the power parents behold,
A kid can only pretend to be so bold,

A kid can never break the mold,
A whirl away from the knife is the only power I behold.

Hold Back

Terrains and rivers that stretch us afar,
The birds in the sky cry aloud;
Recognize our shared pain as an irreversible scar.
With a bustling street hovered by a swarming crowd,
The dampness of destitute overflows my personal jar.
As your distant whispers pierce through my world so loud.

Even if I could just reach out and touch you,
Feel what you feel,
My emerging agony won't transform as untrue.
When your clothes wither off to reveal,
Your raw skin that I alone can pierce through,
I know you won't be anyone's to steal.

Your smoldering breath seeps underneath me,
Despite my repeated plea,
Because I'm aware that I can't hold back.
These thoughts levitate me as I pack,
My clothes, books, our memories,
And I drape our time together with tapestries.

Whenever the time to see you again will arrive,
My paralyzed heart will beat back alive,
Proximity might make our relationship revive,
But I know that first I will flee
As your image brushes my eyes,
Because the intensity I harbour in me,
Will unleash a monster who's dormant in disguise.

Time As A Scar

I am not a famous poet;
Nor am I a famous novelist;
Nor do can I muster up the courage to scream,
But that does not entail the unwavering fact,
That my voice should dissipate as unheard.

I couldn't be by your side.
They wouldn't let me in no matter how hard I tried.
Sneaking in and breaking down the doors to get to you.
I went to the most crowded place in the city,
With a roaring stampede without a mask but with crippling fear.

I wouldn't even care to wash my hands.
I licked them clean, hoping that something would happen to me.
I. Did. Everything.
I wanted to place myself in your pain and misery,
If you couldn't breathe, then what's the point of my existence?

You made me who I am.
What gives me the right to live
While your life gets thrown away?
But in the end, I got dragged away,
And be content with the glass between us.

I banged on the window desperately hoping;
That one of those morons with a self claimed PhDs;
Would understand my suffering and let me in.
But I didn't get to inhale any of your suffering.
While you were trapped without the strength to even lift a finger.

The day that decided the irretrievable fact
That I will never get to you again.
Everyone tells me, "Things will get better"
"Time is the greatest healer there is."
No one guessed that I simply did not wish to heal.

All I want now, is for time to scar me even further,
As your absence begins to gnaw me inside out.

Noon Of My Night

You weren't responsible for me.
As a bachelor, you could live your life free,
Yet, you chose my mother on one knee.
Several years ago, you stood under a tree,
Drinking water like it gushed from the roaring sea;
As the sun flamed with glee.

Past the oak tree, past the aperture of glass,
There lay a little baby in a delicious slumber.
Who knew that as years pass,
This would merely remain a moment to remember.
Time fluttered away and then we first meet;
I saw a loyal man who would never cheat.

The time we spent together,
It never felt like I was on a tether.
The way we discussed the weather;
Or debate upon stumbling on a bird's feather;
Those moments drew you closer to me than my mother.
You cared for me; not seeing me as a child of some other.

As the raindrops poured down the window shield;
And I drove the car on a single-laned highway,
All my secrets were sealed,
Just like how my hands were on the wheel.
Just like how it would snow in June,
You ask me if I was gay.
I never imagined the time would arrive so soon.
If I honestly answered you, I'd be left stray.
I squeaked no; wrapping myself back in a cocoon.
I was afraid to lose the one man who brought noon in the night.

Stories That Sprout

The sensation of thousands waiting,
Bursts in my heart as I casually stroll in.
The products that the authors were creating;
The words fly out of the page, sinking into my skin.
The sounds of the pages turning in a perfect synchrony;
The sound of me scratching my chin in wonder;
All align together to recite in a glorious harmony.
The smile on my face struck me like thunder,
As the books decide to write a spell that I'm under.
I find myself unable to move my feet,
While my mind is engaged in a magnificent fleet.
The owner steps up from his designated counter,
He is someone I don't wish to encounter,
As he will force the idea of paying for a book,
As he will force to tear me away from the thousands,
Of pages who are urging me to have a look.
To read the stories that sprouted in their white land.

A Mere Bypasser

My feet find themselves on a barren land,
Which shares where the skyscrapers stand.
The rain gushed amidst the gleaming lights,
Thus making Halifax one of my favorite sights.
When the world around you seems so galactic,
One believes that their lives will turn climactic.
Where one sees a harmonious breeze,
Where the raindrops and the city lights,
Engage themselves in an enthralling tease,
Remaining in a scene without overthrowing the other.
Behaving like half-brothers, with a single mother nature.

I decide to indulge in this scene, being a mere bypasser.
I blast my headphones with music, not being a trespasser.
I walk by an amazing orchard of autumn trees,
The red and orange leaves do not prefer to freeze,
As they drift along the damp breeze.
Which is why I'm walking home and not taking a cab.
As the musical notes resonate in my ear with a stab,
My footsteps transform into a hurried brisk.
Even when I realize that speeding can be a risk.
I wished for this scene to keep expanding forever,
Let the rain and light continue to fulfill my selfish endeavours.

A Child Is A Parent's Greatest Strength

What does being a parent mean to you?
I could only wish someone would ask me that.
They taunt, what would a 16-year-old know about motherhood?
Boy, people these days do not have a clue.
They say, teenagers are spoilt brats,
But never did they try to understand where I stood.

Even if they are right in their snarky judgements,
Even if they are right in their baseless comments,
Why doesn't a parent ask, what does being a child mean to you?
I'll answer those two, based on what I've been through.

One does not need to deliver a baby or,
Donate millions of sperm to score.
One needs to unconditionally adore,
That little life to their heart's deepest core.
Pick them up if they are sore,
Impart skills by delegating chores,
Bring about a smile when life is a bore,
Yell when they break a promise they swore,
Calm them down when they roar,
And most of all, be the reason why they take a leap and soar.

Do biological aspects of having a child matter?
Would that make yourself easier to flatter?
If you think you're smart, this norm should be yours to shatter.
Now, allow me to answer the latter.

One does not need to come out of their mother's womb,
Or be a result of their father's boom.
One needs to unconditionally love,
The people who took them in and built a life,
Look at those people like figures from the above,

But not afraid of whether they will stab you as a piercing knife.
Once they begin to fear of them,
You are no longer their precious gem.
You begin to drift away.
And the distance merely increases by the day.

Why are parents so afraid to admit to their child?
Why are children so afraid to admit to their parents?
Like all relationships, communication is key.
After all, a child is a parent's greatest strength,
And parents are a child's greatest saviours.

What I Was Pining For

I came here without expecting much.
Wasn't looking for anyone per say.
Already had a best friend as such.
Got bestowed with a lover as clear as day.

But I knew something was missing.

My best friend and I have been through a lot,
Whatever challenges high school brought,
Together we remained and fought.
It would always be like this, or so I thought.

But I knew something was missing.

When I first saw you, I didn't know what to think.
You strolled by in the matter of a blink.
Never did I assume that we'd have a link.
Never did I assume our thoughts would be in sync.

Something in me had begun to change.

Your reactions to the littlest of things caught me off-guard.
With all due honesty, they struck me incredibly hard.
My wounds that were scarred were not merely glossed over.
Your words soothed me like my face was adorned with clover.

Something in me had begun to change.

These feelings stirring up inside of me,
Were considered as romantic love, you see.
My mind became as turbulent as the galactic sea.
But never did I feel such glee.

Eventually, I knew what I found in you.

A humble soul,
Who was timid yet blatantly honest.
Who made me feel like a complete whole.
Who never made even one false promise.
Who never made me like my opinions held value.
Eventually, I found the ONE friend I was pining for.

A Man With Headphones

Whatever it takes, I know I can make it through…
The spark present electric guitar of that song,
Jolts me awake every single day.
My body is instantly filled with adrenaline.
Ready to seize the moments I'll get to have.

When adversity strikes its way upon my path,
The lyrics that are nothing more than simple words,
The singer's voice, that I could probably replicate,
All swarm around my dejected self,
Transforming me, ready to dance to his own tunes.

This is the power of music.
Turns the ailing and the sick,
Into beings striving for a sense of hope.
So they no longer mope to cope.
They gain the strength to climb life's steepest slope.

www.ingramcontent.com/pod-product-compliance
Lightning Source LLC
La Vergne TN
LVHW010934200726